ANIMALS

Bees

by Kevin J. Holmes

Content Consultant:
Gary A. Dunn
Director of Education
Young Entomologists' Society

Bridgestone Books
an imprint of Capstone Press

Bridgestone Books are published by Capstone Press
818 North Willow Street, Mankato, Minnesota 56001
http://www.capstone-press.com

Printed in the United States of America.

Library of Congress Cataloging-in-Publication Data
Holmes, Kevin J.
Bees / by Kevin J. Holmes.
p. cm.--(Animals)
Includes bibliographical references (p. 23) and index.
Summary: An introduction to bees' physical characteristics, habits, behavior, and relationships to humans.
ISBN 1-56065-742-1
1. Bees--Juvenile literature. [1. Bees.] I. Title. II. Series: Holmes, Kevin J. Animals.
QL565.2.H655 1998
595.79'9--dc21

97-31854
CIP
AC

Editorial credits
Editor, Martha E. Hillman; cover design, Timothy Halldin; photo research, Michelle L. Norstad
Photo credits
Dembinsky Photo Assoc. Inc./Ed Kanze, cover
James H. Robinson, 4, 12
James P. Rowan, 8
Visuals Unlimited/Barbara Gerlach, 6; J. Alcock, 10; Richard L. Carlton, 14;
W. Ormerod, 16; R. Williamson, 18; L. J. Connor, 20

Table of Contents

Thorax
Eyes
Antennas
Wings
Abdomen
Legs
Proboscis

Fast Facts

Kinds: There are about 20,000 kinds of bees.

Range: Bees live everywhere in the world except Antarctica.

Habitat: Most bees make nests in trees, plants, or the ground. Some live in homes called hives.

Food: Bees drink nectar and eat pollen. Nectar is a sweet liquid in flowers. Pollen is tiny grains that flowers produce.

Mating: Some bees mate only in the spring. Other bees mate anytime.

Young: Newborn bees are larvas. They hatch from eggs. Larvas turn into pupas. Pupas change into adult bees.

Bees

Bees are insects. An insect is a small animal with a hard outer shell. Insects have six legs and no backbones. Some insects have wings.

There are more than 20,000 kinds of bees in the world. Each bee is a queen bee, a worker bee, or a drone. Queen bees are females. They are the only bees that lay eggs. Worker bees are also female. They take care of young bees. Drones are male bees. They mate with queen bees. Mate means to join together to produce young.

Some bees are social. They live in large communities with many bees. These bees work together. They raise young bees and gather food. They also guard their communities.

Most bees are solitary bees. Solitary means alone. Solitary bees gather food alone. They usually live alone. Solitary bees sometimes build nests near other bees, however.

Most bees are solitary bees.

Appearance

Bees are many colors. Some are black with yellow stripes. Others are brown. Some are green or blue.

Most bees have hair on their bodies. Some have hair on their eyes. Bees use hair to feel objects. Pollen from flowers also sticks to the hair. Pollen is tiny grains that flowers produce.

A bee's body has three parts. The front part is the head. The eyes are on the head. The head also has antennas. Bees use antennas to smell, feel, and taste.

The middle part of a bee's body is the thorax. A bee's legs and wings are part of its thorax.

The back part of a bee's body is the abdomen. Many bees have stingers on their abdomens. Bees use stingers to hurt their enemies. But not all bees have stingers.

Some bees are green.

Homes

Bees live everywhere in the world except Antarctica. Some live in cold places. But most bees live where it is warm. Bees must live near flowers. They get their food from flowers.

Solitary bees build nests in trees or plants. Some build nests in the ground. They sometimes build their nests near each other. They may work together to keep their nests safe from enemies.

Social bees live in hives. They make hives out of beeswax. Bees make beeswax in their bodies. They build hives in trees or on rocks. As many as 50,000 bees live in each hive.

Social bees shape beeswax into small cells inside hives. Queen bees lay eggs in some cells. Worker bees store honey in other cells.

Sometimes a hive will have two queen bees. One queen bee will leave the hive. Many bees from the hive swarm with her. Swarm means a group of bees leaves one hive to form another.

Some solitary bees build nests in the ground.

Food

Bees gather nectar and pollen from flowers. Nectar is a sweet liquid in flowers. Bees drink nectar and eat pollen. They also use pollen and nectar to make honey. Bees make food for young bees with pollen and nectar.

A bee has a proboscis for drinking nectar from flowers. A proboscis is a tongue shaped like a tube.

Bees use the hair on their bodies to gather pollen. The pollen sticks in the hair. Some bees store pollen in pouches on their legs. Bees carry pollen to their nests.

Bees help pollinate flowers. Pollinate means to carry pollen from one flower to another. Pollen helps some flowers turn into fruit. It also helps some flowers make seeds that become new plants.

Bees gather nectar and pollen from flowers.

Enemies

Bees have many enemies. Some enemies eat their honey. Bears sometimes reach into hives to get honey.

Some enemies eat bees. Many birds, toads, and spiders eat bees. Bee stings do not harm them.

Honey badgers and honey guide birds live in Africa and India. The honey guide birds lead honey badgers to bee hives. Honey badgers use their claws to open hives. They eat the honey and young bees. Then the honey guide birds also eat some honey.

Bees sting to guard themselves from enemies. They also sting to guard their nests. Bees sting by putting their stingers into enemies. A small amount of poison flows through the stingers. Their stingers break off when the bees fly away. Most bees die soon after losing their stingers.

Some spiders eat bees.

Communication

Communication is sending and receiving messages. Social bees use movements and scents to communicate.

Some bees communicate by dancing. They dance to let other bees know where flowers are. They give directions with their movements.

Bees also communicate through scents. Worker bees send out scents when hives are in danger. These scents warn other bees to guard their hives. The scent smells like bananas.

Queen bees also give off scents. These scents tell other bees that the queen bees are healthy. Queen bees stop giving off scents when they are sick. This tells worker bees to begin raising new queens and drones. They raise drones to mate with the queens.

Some bees communicate by dancing.

Life Stages

Bees go through four life stages. The stages are egg, larva, pupa, and adult.

Queen bees lay eggs after mating with drones. The drones die soon after mating. Each queen bee mates only one time.

Social queen bees lay many eggs. Some lay up to 1,500 eggs each day. The queen bees lay their eggs in wax cells inside the hive. Worker bees care for the young as they grow.

Solitary queen bees lay eggs in their nests. Some take care of the eggs. Others put pollen near the eggs and leave.

Larvas hatch from eggs. They are bees in the second life stage. Larvas look like worms.

Larvas spin cocoons as they change into pupas. Pupas are bees in the third life stage.

Pupas change into adult bees inside their cocoons. They are fully grown after a few weeks. Then they come out of their cocoons.

Larvas are bees in the second life stage.

Bees and People

Many people are afraid of bee stings. But bees only sting to guard their nests and themselves.

Bees help people in many ways. Bees pollinate flowers and trees. People enjoy the flowers and eat fruit from the trees. Many of these plants could not live without bees.

Honey bees make honey and beeswax. Beekeepers gather the honey and beeswax from hives. A beekeeper is a person who raises honey bees. People eat the honey. They use the beeswax to make candles and crayons.

Some beekeepers bring their bees to fruit farms. The bees pollinate the fruit trees. They collect pollen and nectar from the trees. The bees use the pollen and nectar to make honey.

Beekeepers gather honey and beeswax from hives.

Hands On: Charades

Bees communicate with body movements. You can communicate with movements by playing charades.

What You Need

A group of friends

Paper and a pencil

Animal cards or animal pictures

What You Do

1. Ask each player to choose two animal cards or pictures. The players should not show their cards to each other.
2. Take turns acting like the animal on each card or picture. Do not talk or make animal noises.
3. Have the other players guess what the animal is.
4. Give one point to the first player who guesses the animal. Use the paper and pencil to keep score. The player with the most points wins.

Words to Know

abdomen (AB-duh-muhn)—the back part of a bee's body

beekeeper (BEE-kee-puhr)—a person who raises honey bees

insect (IN-sekt)—a small animal with a hard outer shell and six legs; an insect's body has three parts.

larva (LAR-vah)—a bee in the second life stage; a larva hatches from an egg.

pollen (POL-uhn)—tiny grains that flowers produce

proboscis (pro-BOS-kiss)—a tongue shaped like a tube

pupa (PYOO-pah)—a bee in the third life stage; a pupa grows in a cocoon.

thorax (THOR-aks)—the middle part of a bee's body

Read More

Fisher, Enid. *Bees*. Milwaukee: Gareth Stevens Publishing, 1996.

Hinds, Marcia. *Killer Bees*. Mankato, Minn.: RiverFront Books, 1998.

Useful Addresses

National Honey Board
390 Lashley St.
Longmont, CO 80501-6045

Young Entomologists' Society
1915 Peggy Place
Lansing, MI 48910-2553

Internet Sites

The Insects Home Page
http://www.ex.ac.uk/~gjlramel/six.html
Minibeast Homepage
http://www.tesser.com/minibeast/
Science World: Exhibits: Bees
http://www.schoolnet.ca/collections/science_world/english/exhibits/bees/

Index